The Middle School Survival Manual

KATRINA L. CASSEL

Copyright © 2010 Concordia Publishing House
3558 S. Jefferson Ave., St. Louis, MO 63118-3968
1-800-325-3040 • www.cph.org

Unless otherwise indicated, Scripture quotations are from the ESV Bible® (The Holy Bible, English Standard Version®), copyright © 2001 by Crossway Bibles, a publishing ministry of Good News Publishers. Used by permission. All rights reserved.

Scripture quotations marked NIV are taken from the HOLY BIBLE, NEW INTERNATIONAL VERSION®. NIV®. Copyright © 1973, 1978, 1984 by International Bible Society. Used by permission of Zondervan Publishing House. All rights reserved.

Manufactured in the United States of America

Library of Congress Cataloging-in-Publication Data

Cassel, Katrina L., 1962-
The middle school survival manual / Katrina L. Cassel.
    p. cm.
  ISBN 978-0-7586-1790-3
  1. Middle schools--United States--Handbooks, manuals, etc.--Juvenile litera-
ture. 2. Study skills--United States--Handbooks, manuals, etc.--Juvenile literature.
I. Title.
  LB1623.5.C38 2010
  373.23'6--dc22

1 2 3 4 5 6 7 8 9 10   19 18 17 16 15 14 13 12 11 10

To **Jasmine, Kaleb** and **Kayla**.
Though middle school seems far off, that day will be here all too soon. I pray your middle school years are wonderful as you grow in faith, expand your knowledge, increase your talents, and thrive in all you do!

A special thanks to

Rick: Best friend and guide

Tyler: Firstborn

Jessica: Firstborn princess

Adam: Warrior in the making

Jasmine: My joy and song

And to **Teresa** for reading the manuscript and making suggestions

TABLE OF CONTENTS

INTRODUCTION

Welcome to middle school! These years are full of adventure and excitement, growth and learning. They are also full of change.

Gone are the days when you mostly had one teacher and the same classmates all day. In middle school, you have new classes and possibly a different teacher for each class. You may even get to choose some classes such as band, art, computer, or Spanish. You can explore your talents as you make new friends and try new activities.

Middle school has some unique challenges. You may be changing classes for the first time. You might have to negotiate hallways and a much bigger building, as well as figure out how to open your locker with just minutes between classes. You have more than one teacher assigning homework and projects and giving tests. That might mean tests in several classes all on the same day. Pressure to succeed and peer pressure are more intense. Your faith may be tested.

This book can help you with those challenges. It'll show you how to organize your time, study for and take tests, choose good activities, and more. You'll find Scripture verses to guide you, quizzes to help you discover more about yourself, questions to help you focus on what you learn, and other activities to help you navigate your way through middle school. There are pages at the end of each chapter to help you put what you learn into practice so you'll not only survive, but thrive in your middle school years.

— KATRINA "KATHY" CASSEL

Go for It!

Have you ever set a goal and achieved it? If you have, be proud of yourself. A goal can be as small as reading a book for a book report or as large as winning an award. Doing either of those things is an accomplishment, a step forward. This chapter will help you set realistic goals and make a plan to achieve them.

Brayden ran up the school steps with his backpack slung over one shoulder and his trombone case in hand.

"How was your summer?" his friend Gabe asked.

"Boring as usual. I'm almost glad to be back in school!"

"What? Did I hear you right?" Gabe said.

"Yeah, I guess. I plan to make marching band this year," Brayden said.

"You been practicing this summer?" Gabe asked.

"Taking private lessons and practicing. That's the only way to reach my goal."

Brayden set his trombone down and looked at his schedule. He was in the right building for homeroom. That was a good start.

"I guess goals aren't my thing," Gabe said. "I don't have any idea what I want to do this year. I guess passing pre-algebra would be enough for me."

Brayden turned to face Gabe. "Passing pre-algebra is a goal—and a good one. We can work on it together."

The warning bell sounded, interrupting the conversation. Brayden and Gabe raced for homeroom together.

YOUR TURN!

Someone once said, "He who aims for nothing always achieves it." That's certainly true. Doing nothing is easy. But if you have plans for yourself—like being a pro skateboarder, making the football team, or, like Gabe, passing pre-algebra—then you need to set some goals. Goals help you focus on what you want to do and on what is most important. You can start making and achieving goals now. The following steps will help you to set some goals for yourself this school year.

THINK ABOUT WHAT YOU WANT TO ACCOMPLISH

What's important to you? What new skills would you like to learn? Are there areas in your life that could use some improvement? Goals can help! Do old habits need breaking, or does a new habit need to be formed? Are there skills you want to improve? Do you want to make more friends or better grades? Set some goals today!

Here are some areas where you might want to set goals:

★ **Music**

★ **Sports and fitness**

★ **Drama or performing arts**

★ **Spiritual growth**

★ **Relationships**

★ **Grades and test taking**

★ **Even electronic games and hobbies!**

CHOOSE ONE OR TWO THINGS THAT INTEREST YOU THE MOST

Limiting your choices allows you to give more time and energy to the things that are most important to you. You may decide to improve your grades and your fitness level or to do better in your relationships with God and your family. Decide which areas are priorities. You can always change your mind or add new choices later as you meet your goals.

SET ONE OR TWO SPECIFIC GOALS

Many people make New Year's resolutions but fail to keep them. The problem is that resolutions are too general. "I will exercise" or "I will read my Bible" are good resolutions, but if there isn't a plan, it probably won't happen. Be specific.

★ **Know what you want to accomplish.** Write it down in a couple of sentences.

★ **Why is the goal important to you?** How will it improve your life or help others?

★ **What does it look like when it's finished?** If your goal is to be a faster runner, what is the end point? Does that mean you will run a mile in seven minutes? six minutes? Does that mean you will be the fastest runner on the track team?

TALK TO GOD ABOUT YOUR GOALS

God has a plan for you. You aren't an accident. You aren't a failure. God knew you before you were born, and He has something He wants you to accomplish. There are things He plans for you to do and people He wants you to reach.

God promises to give you the strength to do the things you are meant to do. Philippians 4:13 says, "I can do all things through Him who strengthens me." God will help you accomplish His plan in your life. Ask Him what goals He wants you to achieve.

MAKE A GAME PLAN

Once you know what you want to accomplish, you need a plan. Follow a step-by-step map to completion.

1. Ask yourself, "What is my end point for this goal? What do I need to do to get to that point?" Suppose you want a B in history. You need at least a score of 80 percent. Right now, your overall score for homework, quizzes, and tests is 60 percent. To achieve your goal, you must raise your grade 20 percent. Or maybe your end goal is to complete the obstacle course in gym class in less than three minutes. Right now, it takes you four and one-half minutes. You need to improve your time by 90 seconds. Think about what you want to do and what it will take to get you there.

2. List some specific things you can do to reach that goal. To get the B in history, you might need to take notes that are more thorough, listen better in class, review the material each night, or study with a friend. To get faster at the obstacle course, you might try to get more sleep and eat healthier food so you feel more energetic. Practice the areas that are most challenging, and work with a friend who can give you pointers to improve your performance.

3. Organize your ideas into a plan. List your ideas step-by-step in the order you plan to do them. Be specific about each step. Here is a sample plan for improving your history test grade:

★ Listen in class.

★ Take notes and review them each night.

★ Read the textbook assignments and add important information to class notes.

★ Once the test is announced, spend twenty minutes a night studying notes and memorizing details.

★ Spend an hour on Saturday reviewing with a friend or having a parent quiz you.

A plan for improving your time on the obstacle course might look like this:

★ Replace junk food with fruits and vegetables.

★ Sleep eight hours a night.

★ Spend thirty minutes a night on challenging areas of the obstacle course.

★ Practice with a friend one night a week.

★ Time myself once a week and chart improvement.

4. Put the plan into action. Start now and work on it a little bit every day. Don't try to do it all at once, or you might burn out and give up. Just work toward the goal a little bit at a time, and you should see steady progress.

CHECK YOUR PROGRESS

Each week or month, check how close you are to reaching your goal. Ask yourself:

★ Is my goal realistic?

★ Is my game plan working?

★ Am I closer to my goal today than when I started? than a month ago? than last week?

★ Am I still interested in achieving this goal?

Check your progress for each goal and decide if it's going well or not. You can change your game plan if you aren't progressing well or if you don't have the time or interest you first had for your goal. Changing your plan doesn't mean you've failed. It will keep you from giving up in despair. And don't forget to celebrate when you achieve your goal.

So set some goals today and make a game plan. Find a friend to work with to make it more fun. You'll be surprised at all you can accomplish!

Just Do It!

Now it's time for you to put what you've just learned into action. It's not enough to just read about it, you have to do it to accomplish anything. So here we go.

THINK ABOUT WHAT YOU WANT TO ACCOMPLISH

Listed below are several general areas in which you might want to improve. Put an X beside each one you that interests you, or add areas of your own.

- ○ Improve your grades
- ○ Do art projects
- ○ Break bad habits
- ☒ Grow in faith
- ☒ Improve your fitness level
- ☒ Improve musically
- ○ Work on family relationships (talk to parents more, spend time with family, get to know siblings better)
- ○ Make new friends
- ○ Get along better with teachers

○ Learn a new sport or improve at one you already play

○ Learn new study skills

○ Participate in community service

CHOOSE ONE OR TWO THINGS THAT INTEREST YOU THE MOST

Which areas for improvement are most important to you at this particular time? Go back and circle one or two areas from the list.

SET ONE OR TWO SPECIFIC GOALS

Write goals that interest you the most.

TALK TO GOD ABOUT YOUR GOALS

Read James 1:5. What does it say about wisdom?

Read Philippians 4:13. How does it apply to accomplishing your goals?

MAKE A GAME PLAN

Setting a goal is great, but you need to know how you will achieve it. Make a list of things you can do to achieve the two goals you wrote above.

Goal #1 game plan:

A.

B.

C.

Goal #2 game plan:

A.

B.

C.

CHECK YOUR PROGRESS

In a week, reread your goals and review your game plan. Do the same in a month.

- ★ Is your goal doable?

- ★ Do you still want to achieve it?

- ★ Is your game plan working? If not, what needs to be changed?

- ★ Are you closer to reaching your goal than you were a week ago?

REVISE YOUR GOALS AS NEEDED

Once you've completed a goal, write another one to replace it. Aim high and pray about your goals. With God's help, you can accomplish great things!

VERSES TO THINK ABOUT

Think about these verses this week. Consider memorizing them so they'll always be in your heart.

Trust in the LORD with all your heart, and do not lean on your own understanding. In all your ways acknowledge Him, and He will make your paths straight. **Proverbs 3:5–6**

For I know the plans I have for you, declares the LORD, plans for welfare and not for evil, to give you a future and a hope. **Jeremiah 29:11**

CHAPTER
TWO

Give Your Grades a Boost

Does report card day leave you feeling discouraged—and in trouble with your parents? Do you ever wish there were more A's or B's on your report card or that it wasn't so hard to get the grades you want? This chapter will teach you study skills to give your grades a boost. Even if you already get A's and B's, you may find some new study tips to try.

> *Daniel studied the grades on his report card. The only A was in Phys Ed. That wouldn't impress his parents. The B in history wasn't bad either, but the C's and D's in the rest of his classes were sure to lose him his electronic game system for a month.*

Daniel folded up the report card and stuffed it into his pocket. He'd throw it in the trash, but his parents would find out sooner or later. He knew he was in for the "You're not working up to your potential" speech, as well as the loss of privileges. Daniel just wasn't sure that he had the potential his parents and teachers seemed to see in him. And it wasn't that he wasn't trying—he was. But even when he thought he was doing well, his grades still fell short.

YOUR TURN!

Do your grades fall short of what you hope for? Have you ever wondered if grades really matter? God probably doesn't look at the grades recorded on your report card, but He does care about the work you do! Getting good grades is easier for some students than for others, but *all* students can improve their study skills—and their grades.

HOW DO YOU RATE?

Read the sentences below. Then mark *Always*, *Sometimes*, or *Never* for each one.

1. I have all the supplies and books I need when I arrive at my classroom.

preparation

   ○ Always   ○ Sometimes   ○ Never

2. I listen in class, even when it's boring.

participation

   ○ Always   ○ Sometimes   ○ Never

3. I try to relate the things the teacher says to things I already know.

○ Always   ○ Sometimes   ○ Never

4. I have a system for taking notes that works for me.

○ Always   ○ Sometimes   ○ Never

5. I do my homework while I still feel alert and energetic.

○ Always   ○ Sometimes   ○ Never

6. I study for tests a little bit each night.

○ Always   ○ Sometimes   ○ Never

7. My parents and friends are willing to help me with my schoolwork.

○ Always   ○ Sometimes   ○ Never

YES!

   If you marked *Always* for all the sentences above, then you probably don't need this chapter. But if you marked *Sometimes* or *Never*, then you have work to do. So let's get started. Remember, God has made you His child, so "Whatever your hand finds to do, do it with your might" (Ecclesiastes 9:10). God judges whether you are doing your best, not the grade on your report card.

   Here are some steps to help you be more successful in class:

BE PREPARED

   You probably know students who arrive late to class without their textbooks, paper, pens, or homework. They aren't prepared! But having your supplies and homework is only part of being ready.

Being prepared also involves being familiar with the things you've already learned in class. Review your notes every night. Look ahead in your textbook. What will you be learning in the next few weeks?

If you do this, you'll arrive at class with the material fresh in your mind, ready to participate in class discussions.

LISTEN EFFECTIVELY

You spend more time listening than you spend reading, writing, or talking. Most of your school day is spent listening, but *effective* listening goes beyond just hearing the words. You need to concentrate on what's said and also understand it.

How much do you really know about listening? Take the quiz below to find out.

1. It's important to know whether you're listening to understand directions, to learn something new, or for another reason.

_____ True   _____ False

2. The average person does which of the following?

   a. Speaks about 500 words a minute but can hear and understand about 150 words a minute.

   b. Speaks about 135 words a minute but can hear and understand about 500 words a minute.

   c. Speaks about 330 words a minute and can hear and understand about 330 words a minute.

3. In class it's important to do which of the following?

   a. Listen for both concepts and details.

b. Listen for the big picture and forget the details.

c. Concentrate on the details that might be on the test.

4. If you're <u>bored or confused while your teacher is talking</u>, what should you do?

a. Text your best friend.

b. Listen for new information and relate it to what you already know.

c. Make your to-do list for after school.

d. Write down questions to ask the teacher later.

Answers:

1. True. You can relax when you're hearing a funny story or a joke, but when you're hearing instructions you need to listen for step-by-step details. If you're learning new material, you have to listen to understand concepts. Knowing why you're listening can help you tune in better.

2. B: The average person speaks about 135 words per minute and can hear and understand almost 500 words per minute. Since you process information faster than your teacher speaks, it's easy to let your mind wander. *Don't!* Use that time to think through what the teacher is saying and relate it to things you already know. Think about questions you may have about the information.

3. A: Sometimes you can focus on details and miss major concepts. You may be so caught up in the details of a war that you miss why the war took place in the first place. Or you might listen for concepts and miss important details. Tie facts and concepts together in your mind while your teacher is talking.

4. B and D: It's hard to keep listening when you don't understand the material or are bored. Listen for things you do understand and for interesting pieces of information. Make note of what you need the teacher to clarify.

Listening involves more than hearing words. It requires thinking through and organizing information in your mind.

TAKE NOTES

Do you have trouble knowing how much or how little to write down in class? Is it difficult to know what is really important? Try these ideas:

★ **Jot down key words and phrases.** Don't try to record word for word what your teacher says. Use abbreviations whenever possible.

★ **Follow along in your book.** If your teacher starts listing the reasons for the Civil War, jot down the page number in your textbook. Write down extra information your teacher gives.

★ **Listen for key phrases.** Comments like "The causes are . . ." or "The significance of the events were . . ." let you know the teacher is about to give important information.

★ **Ask your teacher for note-taking suggestions.** He or she knows what is most important, so don't be afraid to ask for advice.

★ **Review your notes as soon as possible.** Organize your notes and add information from the textbook. Read your notes aloud. This helps you remember the information longer and be more organized when it's time to study for the test. There will be more about learning styles and studying for tests in the next chapter.

DO ALL ASSIGNMENTS

★ **Write down your homework.** Many schools give out a planner at the beginning of the year to keep track of homework and tests. If your school provides a planner, use it. If not, divide a piece of notebook paper into columns with these headings: Date, Class, Assignment, Date Due, Done, and Grade. Put a check in the done column as you complete each assignment. Be sure to record the grade you received to monitor your progress. There is a sample page in the "Just Do It" section.

★ **Have a regular time and place for homework.** Don't let instant messaging, texting, phone calls, or anything else interrupt you. Some people study better with music in the background, while others need it quiet. Do what works for you. Organize your materials first so that once you begin, you won't waste study time looking for books, pens, and paper.

★ **Start with the hardest assignment first.** Do the assignment you least want to do while you feel fresh. Work until it's completely done, and then check it off on your assignment list. Take breaks between assignments. Leave the easiest assignments for last when you least feel like doing homework.

READ EFFECTIVELY

Do you have a lot of assigned reading? If you do, you need to develop a plan of attack to make your reading easier and more useful. Try these suggestions:

★ **Preview first.** Whether you have to read an entire chapter or just a section of it, skim it first. Look at the headings (words in bold print that start each section). Look at pictures and read the captions. Notice any graphs. Read the questions at the beginning or end of the chapter to help you know what to look for when you read. Look for underlined or italicized words.

★ **Make it a question.** Begin reading a section at a time. Turn the heading into a question. "Causes for the Battle of Gettysburg" becomes "What were the causes for the Battle of Gettysburg?" If the title is "Natural Elements in Our World," ask yourself, "What are the natural elements in our world?" As you read, look for the answer to your question.

★ **Summarize.** List key points or major themes from your reading. Outline what you've read to help you organize information in your mind and remember it longer.

★ **Analyze.** Go a step farther and analyze the material. Is it fact or the author's opinion? Does it agree with what you know and believe?

START PROJECTS EARLY

Avoid last-minute panic by beginning work right away on essays, book reports, science projects, and other long-term projects.

★ **Choose your topic.** Get on the Internet the same day you receive an assignment. Jot down a list of possible topics and find out how many articles are available about each one. Decide which topic suits you best.

★ **Make a time schedule.** Use a calendar to plan. Circle the project's due date, and then plan your strategy. Mark out days for research, writing the paper or doing the project, revising it, and running the final copy.

★ **Set aside time daily.** Allow a certain amount of time every night to work on your project to keep yourself on schedule. You may want to spend less time on weeknights and more time on weekends. Plan whatever works best for you.

ASK QUESTIONS AND GET EXTRA HELP

If you don't understand some of the classroom material, ask questions. If you have trouble with an algebra equation, ask your teacher to demonstrate more problems. Keep asking until you understand. If you find yourself leaving class each day wondering what your teacher was talking about, ask for help from the teacher. Don't hesitate to get the answers you need.

Talk to your parents about problems you have with class work or homework. Your mom, dad, or an older sibling might be able to help you understand your math problem or help you get started on your English essay.

Try these study tips, and watch your grades go up!

Just Do It!

How do your study skills measure up? Ask God for wisdom and help in making needed improvements.

BE PREPARED

Are you prepared to face class each day? Check all the phrases that describe your normal class preparations.

○ Homework done and ready to hand in

○ Class notes reviewed from the previous day

○ Supplies and textbooks placed in a location where they won't be forgotten

Make a plan to fix any areas you could not check.

LISTEN EFFECTIVELY

Go back and see how you did on the listening quiz. In what area do you most need to improve?

TAKE NOTES

Keep these key ideas in mind:

★ Jot down key words and phrases.

★ Listen for key phrases.

★ Recopy your notes nightly.

★ Find someone who takes good notes. Compare them with yours to see what you've missed.

DO ALL ASSIGNMENTS

Make a page in your notebook like this:

DATE	CLASS	ASSIGNMENT	DATE DUE	DONE	GRADE
1.					
2.					
3.					
4.					
5.					
6.					
7.					
8.					
9.					
10.					

List all assignments. If you have overdue assignments, see if the teacher will accept them late for partial credit. If not, do them for your own sake. Skipping them may mean missing important information.

READ EFFECTIVELY

Do you have a lot of reading to catch up on? Keep these important steps in mind:

* ★ Preview first

* ★ Make a question out of it

* ★ Summarize

* ★ Analyze

START PROJECTS EARLY

It's easy to procrastinate on projects—especially if it's one you don't particularly like. Start any upcoming projects *today*.

Find a calendar and circle the due date of the report or project. Now mark off days for researching, for writing the paper or building the science project, for revising or fixing it, and for printing the final copy or building your display.

ASK QUESTIONS AND GET EXTRA HELP

Are you having trouble with a certain subject or with schoolwork in general? Here are some things you can do:

★ **Talk to your guidance counselor**

★ **Ask your teacher for extra help after school**

★ **Talk to your parents about getting you a tutor**

★ **Arrange to study with another student or friend**

Don't ignore problems. They probably won't go away—they'll get worse!

VERSES TO THINK ABOUT

The beginning of wisdom is this: Get wisdom, and whatever you get, get insight. **Proverbs 4:7**

Whatever your hand finds to do, do it with your might. **Ecclesiastes 9:10**

And whatever you do, in word or deed, do everything in the name of the Lord Jesus, giving thanks to God the Father through Him. . . . Whatever you do, work heartily, as for the Lord and not for men. **Colossians 3:17, 23**

And it is my prayer that your love may abound more and more, with knowledge and all discernment, so that you may approve what is excellent, and so be pure and blameless for the day of Christ, filled with the fruit of righteousness that comes through Jesus Christ, to the glory and praise of God. **Philippians 1:9–11**

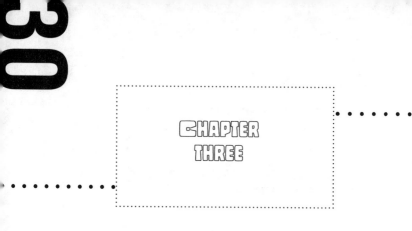

CHAPTER
THREE

Testing
1, 2, 3

Do you know how to study for and take a test? Have you studied for a test but failed it anyway? Do you feel nervous or sick when it's time to take a test? Knowing how to study for and take a test will give you confidence and help raise your scores.

Alexis looked at the history test in front of her. Had she studied the right chapter? None of the questions made any sense. She'd read the material and studied her notes, although she hadn't really taken many notes on this chapter. Still, she thought she'd studied enough.

Alexis was tempted to turn the test in blank but figured she could at least guess on the multiple choice questions. And she had a 50-50 chance on the true and false ones. But she had no hope on the essay questions.

When the bell rang at the end of class, Alexis dropped her test on the teacher's desk and left the room. It was going to be a long year.

YOUR TURN!

Do you ever feel like Alexis? You study, but it just doesn't pay off on the test. If so, this chapter is for you. You'll learn some study and test-taking strategies that are sure to help. And even if you do well on tests, this chapter will teach you about different learning styles, show you the best way for you to learn and retain information and help you study more effectively.

HOW DO YOU BEST LEARN?

Not everyone processes information the same way. Some people learn best by seeing concepts and information. They are visual learners. Others learn best by hearing the material. They are auditory learners. Some students learn best by hands-on learning or by doing. They are kinesthetic learners. How do you best learn? Take the quiz below to find out.

1. You have to give a book report. Would you rather

    a. write it out?

    b. give it orally?

    c. act it out?

2. You're trying to find your way around your new school. Would you learn your way around best by

    a. following a map?

    b. having someone tell you how to get to your classes?

    c. having a guide walk you around school the first day?

3. You have to memorize how many protons and electrons are in certain elements. You would

    a. draw it or study a drawing so you can see the element.

    b. say the number of protons and electrons aloud until you learn it.

    c. make a drawing or model of the protons and electrons so you can get the feel of it.

4. If you can choose your own seat in class, you

    a. sit near the front, where you can see everything.

    b. don't care if you can see the board or screen as long as you can hear what's being said.

    c. sit where you have room to move around.

5. Your class is at the science museum for a field trip. The first thing you do is

    a. find a map so you can see what's there and make a plan.

    b. listen to a guide explain each exhibit and make your plan.

    c. find an exhibit where you can build something.

Check yourself.

If you circled **mostly A's,** you are probably a visual learner.

If you circled **mostly B's**, you are probably an auditory learner.

If you circled **mostly C's**, you are probably a kinesthetic learner.

What does that mean for you?

If you are visual, you learn best by seeing things. You may find it helpful to take detailed notes, make flashcards of vocabulary words or other facts you need to memorize and use diagrams and charts to learn new information. Color-coding new material or tricky spelling words (highlight all the silent letters in yellow) may help you learn better. When a test comes around, you can see the material in your mind.

If you are auditory, you learn best by hearing things. You'd probably rather listen to a book on tape than read the book. It's easier for you to understand things when a teacher explains new material rather than reading it in your textbook. It might help you to read things aloud or have a parent read them to you. Make up a song to a tune you know or create a rap to learn your presidents or state capitols. You memorize best by saying (singing or rapping) things over and over until you've got them. On test day, you can hear the answer in your mind.

If you are kinesthetic, you remember what was done better than what you read or heard. Much of the learning you did in preschool and kindergarten was hands on. You used counters to do math, mixed colors together to see what would happen and got to act out stories. The chances to do hands on activities lessen as you get older. You may need to be creative. Make up hand motions to memorize key facts, draw them or act them out. When test day comes, you'll remember what you did better than what you read.

> *No matter which kind of learner you are, if you can use ideas from all three to help you learn the material, you'll remember it much longer.*

START EARLY

Knowing how you learn best is helpful, but you still have to make time to study. It's best to study a little each night rather than trying to do it all the night before the test.

If you are having trouble, ask for help right away. Don't wait until just before the test to get help. That doesn't leave you enough time to study and prepare.

Study with a friend who understands the information. Quiz each other on the material.

Use what you learned about being a visual, auditory or kinesthetic learner to help. Write your Spanish verbs or science element abbreviations on cards to memorize them. Or make up a rap and say it aloud to learn them. Try saying the verbs while bouncing a basketball. Say the Spanish verb on the first bounce and the English verb on the second.

KNOW WHAT TO EXPECT ON EACH TEST

Which chapters are covered on the test? Will the questions be essay, short answer, or multiple choice?

> ★ **For short-answer or essay tests, know the concepts covered in the chapter.** Have an

overview of the material in your mind. Understand significant events, people, theories, and concepts and how they relate to one another.

★ **For multiple choice or true-or-false tests, pay additional attention to details such as dates, names, places, equations, titles, and authors.**

Even though your teacher has probably given you a study guide, it may help to ask specific questions in the areas where you are having trouble remembering the information.

START THE TEST DAY OUT RIGHT

★ **Try to sleep eight hours the night before a major test.** You'll need a clear mind.

★ **Eat a nutritious breakfast.** Too much sugar can hinder clear thinking.

★ **Pray for wisdom and calmness.**

★ **Get to class a couple of minutes early so you're not in a rush.**

PLAN YOUR STRATEGY

You can study faithfully and still do poorly on a test. Why? It's easy to get nervous and forget what you've learned.

★ **Try to relax as you go into the test.** You've studied and the material is in your mind. Once the test starts, listen to the instructions and read the directions for yourself. Know exactly what the question is asking before you attempt to answer.

★ **Essay test: Read the question and decide what is needed to answer it.** Are you writing about a person's life or just one accomplishment? Are you summarizing a story or analyzing it? Jot down your thoughts. Arrange them in a logical sequence before you begin to write. Include only what is needed to answer the question.

★ **Short-answer test: Follow the same steps as the essay test but make sure your answer is brief and concise.**

★ **Multiple-choice and true-or-false tests: Normally one answer is right, and the others are wrong unless your teacher likes to get tricky and have more than one right answer on multiple-choice tests.** Read the question and have the answer in your mind before you read the choices. Does another answer on the test paper match it? If not, eliminate obvious wrong answers, then choose the best answer left. For a true-or-false test, read the statement. Make sure you read it correctly. If you aren't sure of the answer, try reversing the answer and see how it sounds to you.

★ **Matching test: Read both sides of the test first.** Then read down the left side. Have an answer in mind before searching the right side for a match. Do the ones you know first, then do your best to make logical matches for the others.

★ **Open-book tests: Study the material as thoroughly as you would for any other test.** Write your answers from memory, then use the book to check your answers and fill in what you don't know. Be familiar with the chapter organization so you can quickly find additional information you need.

RECHECK YOUR TEST

Make sure you've answered all of the questions. It's better to guess and have a chance at getting some points than not try at all. Blank spaces won't get you any credit.

Reread the test. Did you mark the answers you intended? Did you answer each question thoroughly? Is your writing legible?

OVERCOMING TEST-DAY JITTERS

Everyone reacts differently to tests. Some students have a mild case of the butterflies. A few students become so nervous they can't function normally. If that's true for you, talk to your guidance counselor or teacher. They can help you deal with test anxiety. Otherwise, you can try these ideas to help you overcome test-day nervousness.

★ **Be so thoroughly prepared you don't have to worry about anything.** Face the test confident that you're ready. Remind yourself that you know the material and will do well on the test. Be confident that God is with you, helping you to remember what you've learned and calming your fears.

★ **If your mind goes blank, don't panic!** Reread the question. Look for key words. Jot down anything that comes to mind and go on to the next question. Try to visualize your notes or hear the teacher in your mind. Draw it out in the margin if you need to.

REVIEW YOUR TEST PERFORMANCE

After the test, review how you did and think of ways to improve your study or test approach. When you get your test back, you can see areas to improve before the next test.

Test day doesn't have to mean failure. Prepare well, approach the test confidently, and do your best!

Just Do It!

Are you a visual, auditory, or kinesthetic learner? Knowing the answer to this question will help you know how to study better. If you aren't sure or if you think you might be a combination of the three, use all of them to help you learn.

Pretend the school-wide spelling bee is approaching. Your teacher just gave you a monstrous list of words to learn. How will you do it? One suggestion is given for each learning style. Add at least one more of your own.

Visual—look at the word, cover it, and try to spell it. Look at it again to see if you got it right.

Your ideas:

Auditory—spell the word aloud looking at the list, cover it and try to spell the word aloud again. Check if you got it right. (Remember that using a tape recorder may be helpful.)

Your ideas:

Kinesthetic—Tap out each letter with a pencil as you say it. Then try to tap it again spelling it by memory. Check your answer.

Your ideas:

Remember to write down test dates in your planner. Then start studying several days ahead.

For the LORD gives wisdom; from His mouth come knowledge and understanding. **Proverbs 2:6**

Blessed is the one who finds wisdom, and the one who gets understanding. **Proverbs 3:13**

For wisdom is better than jewels, and all that you may desire cannot compare with her.
Proverbs 8:11

How much better to get wisdom than gold! To get understanding is to be chosen rather than silver.
Proverbs 16:16

Time Flies

Do you have trouble making time for everything you need to do? Do you try to do too much and not have enough time for any of it? Do you put things off until the last minute? This chapter will help you organize your activities and make the best use of the time you have.

Cody glanced at the clock on his desk. It couldn't be 10:00 already. It was his bedtime and he was only half way through the book he needed to read for his book report. It was due tomorrow, and he still had to write the report after he finished reading. Cody flipped to the end. There were 251 pages and he was on page 119. He groaned.

Cody got up and turned off his room light. He shut his door and turned on his small

desk lamp, hoping his parents wouldn't notice it if they walked by. He'd meant to start the book as soon as it was assigned last month but there were too many others things to do—soccer games, youth group, band practice, and more. He had also spent time with his friends at the skate park and shooting hoops. Cody didn't want to give any of it up, but he knew he had to work on starting projects and homework earlier.

YOUR TURN!

Time can't be recycled. It's never regained. Plan ahead to make the most of your time. By organizing, you will get more done and have more time for yourself. Learning to manage minutes now will save you a lot of stress in the future.

DO YOU PROCRASTINATE?

Do you put things off rather than starting them when you should? Or do you tackle them right away? Take the quiz below to see how you rate. Read the sentence and circle the letter that sounds most like you.

1. Your dad tells you that you have to clean out and sweep the garage before you go to your baseball game on Saturday. You

      a. do it that same day.

      b. do a little bit each day until it's done.

      c. do it Saturday morning right before the game.

      d. don't finish it and miss the game.

2. Your best friend is having a party. She collects anything with butterflies on it. You

> a. have your mom drive you to the mall so you can start searching for butterfly jewelry.
>
> b. go to the mall the night before the party to look for butterfly jewelry.
>
> c. stop by your favorite store on the way to the party and get her anything she might like.
>
> d. make her a card in the car on the way to the party.

3. Your teacher assigned double math homework because everyone was talking in class. You

> a. start it right after school so you'll be done in time.
>
> b. do some of it, then take a break on your computer before finishing it.
>
> c. finish it on the way to school the next morning.
>
> d. don't do it; you have other things to do.

4. It's Friday, and the teacher assigns a biography to read with a report on it due the next Friday. You

> a. read the book and write the report over the weekend.
>
> b. read a couple of chapters a day and write the report Thursday evening.
>
> c. read the book Thursday evening and finish the report on the way to school Friday.
>
> d. hate to read and skip this assignment.

5. Soccer tryouts are next week. When do you start practicing for them?

    a. Start? You've been practicing for a month.

    b. You start right now.

    c. You plan to start in a couple of days.

    d. Practice? Your skills don't need any work.

How did you do?

If you circled **mostly A's**, you are right on top of things, maybe a little too on top of things at times. Relax and allow yourself to be human. It's good that you want to get things done on time, but take time for breaks and fun.

If you circled **mostly B's**, you most often get things done on time. You may not start the minute an assignment is given, but you try to give yourself time to do it. Use a calendar or planner to make sure you are allowing enough time.

If you circled **mostly C's**, you are putting things off too long. It's best to break projects and tasks into smaller chunks and do a little each day. Set small goals and reward yourself for meeting them.

If you circled **mostly D's**, it's time for major change! Write down everything that you need to do and start working your way through the list. Putting off tasks or not doing them at all can only lead to trouble.

GETTING STARTED

If you have trouble finding time to do everything, take a look at what all you are trying to accomplish. Make a list of everything that demands your time. You may be surprised at how much you are trying to fit in a twenty-four hour period!

Include these items:

- ★ **Church**
- ★ **Youth group activities**
- ★ **Homework**
- ★ **Club meetings**
- ★ **Responsibilities at home**
- ★ **Sports practice**
- ★ **Music lessons and practice time**
- ★ **Dance, gymnastics, art, or other special classes**
- ★ **Hobbies**
- ★ **Volunteering**
- ★ **Baby-sitting**
- ★ **Special times with friends**

MAKE A WRITTEN TIME SCHEDULE

By putting an hourly schedule on paper, a calendar, or an electronic planner, you will be able to plan your time more efficiently. To plan on paper, write the days of the week across the top and the hours down the side. There is a sample schedule in the "Just Do It" section.

> ★ **Pray about your priorities.** God can help you decide what most deserves your time. Remember to give God top priority. When Jesus was on earth, He thought it was important to spend time talking

to God. Your heavenly Father knows the many demands on your time. He can give you the wisdom to make good choices about your time.

★ **Schedule "must-do" things first.** Those are church, school and other essential activities that meet at a certain time each day or week. Write those on your schedule in the correct spot.

★ **Add extra-curricular activities, clubs, and sports events that meet at a certain time each week.**

★ **Schedule activities that need to be done but not necessarily at a certain time.** These may include piano practice, homework, and household jobs.

★ **You should have plenty of blank space left on your calendar or planner.** If not, you are trying to do too much. Use the remaining time for activities you wish to do, such as time with friends, television, or reading.

KEEP UP TO DATE

Schedule a little time each day for assignments, projects, and jobs. Breaking projects, assignments, and jobs into smaller tasks makes them more manageable.

If your mom tells you to have your room cleaned by your baseball game Saturday, don't wait until that morning. Pick up all your clothes, books, and other things laying around one day, dust and vacuum the next, organize your closet the following day, and so on. Then keep the room tidied up each day, and it won't be a big job next time.

The same is true for school projects. If you have to do a science fair project, look for a fun and interesting project right away. Once you have it approved by the teacher, start gathering supplies and working on it a little each day. Leave time at the end to do your report and display board.

START EARLY

Start long projects early. Choose a topic for your history paper as soon as it is assigned. Begin researching to avoid rushing or staying up late the night before the essay is due. You can relax as you work, knowing you have a good start and plenty of time.

ORGANIZE

You will save time if you gather and organize your materials at the beginning of each work session. Locate books, pens, and notes first. Once you've organized, begin work and complete the tasks at hand.

DO IT ANYWAY

Some days you probably don't feel like doing your math or science homework. Or you may not want to clean your room or walk the dog. The best thing is to just do it. You may spend an hour texting or online avoiding it, but you'll still have to do it later. Do it first and look forward to a fun break later.

Top Time Wasters

The important thing is not to let any one of these have too much of your time. It's best to set a limit and use a timer to remind yourself.

Television. Set a time limit for yourself. Choose which shows you really want to watch. Turn the television off when they are over.

Video/electronic games. Use gaming as a reward when your homework is done. It's easy to start playing your favorite game and lose track of time, so be careful to keep an eye on the clock.

Phone. It's fun to talk about your day with a friend, but a five-minute call can easily turn into an hour-long chat session. Reward yourself with a fifteen-minute calling or text-messaging time when your hardest assignment is done.

The Net. You can lose yourself in social networking online. By time you check all your favorites, the evening may have passed without you doing any of your homework. Set aside a certain amount of time when your homework is done.

GET HELP

If you are really trying to organize and use your time well but nothing you do seems to help you get caught up or stay on task, talk to a parent or your school counselor. Perhaps there is a reason for your frustration—and a solution. You may be trying to do too much or not getting enough sleep. Or maybe the work is too hard for you. Talk to someone about it.

PLAN LEISURE TIME

Your schoolwork and other responsibilities are important, but include fun time too. Plan a trip to the mall with a friend or a workout on the basketball court to help you think clearly. Trying to go full speed without a break leads to burnout, and you won't have the desire or energy to do your best.

Put these time-saving steps in practice today, and you will be surprised at how much you can accomplish!

Just Do It!

Time to get organized! Have you put off projects? Have you neglected a task? Is homework long overdue? List everything that is overdue or that you've been avoiding.

❏   1.

❏   2.

❏   3.

❏   4.

❏   5.

Start with item one and work until completed. Check the line, and go to the next item. Continue until you've completed the list.

Make a time schedule using the chart on the next page.

Block out times you are at school and church.

★ **Fill in sports practices, clubs, and other activities that meet at a certain time daily or weekly.**

★ **Budget time for your jobs at home, homework, long-term projects, music practice, and other obligations.**

★ **Schedule at least two periods of two hours each a week for leisure time.** Plan to make the most of it!

★ **Stick to the schedule for a month, then revise as needed.** Update your schedule as demands for priorities and time change.

	SUNDAY	MONDAY	TUESDAY	WEDNESDAY	THURSDAY	FRIDAY	SATURDAY
6 a.m.							
7 a.m.							
8 a.m.							
9 a.m.							
10 a.m.							
11 a.m.							
noon							
1 p.m.							
2 p.m.							
3 p.m.							
4 p.m.							
5 p.m.							
6 p.m.							
7 p.m.							
8 p.m.							
9 p.m.							
10 p.m.							

VERSES TO THINK ABOUT

My times are in Your hand. **Psalm 31:15a**

For everything there is a season, and a time for every matter under heaven. **Ecclesiastes 3:1**

But seek first the kingdom of God and His righteousness, and all these things will be added to you. **Matthew 6:33**

Facing a New School

Attending a new school means making new friends, navigating an unfamiliar building, and adjusting to different teachers and a new schedule. You may face a change of schools because you've moved to another neighborhood or state, or because of the transition from elementary school to middle school. If you will be starting at a new school, this chapter will give you tips for adjusting.

Lauren fumbled with her locker combination, willing it to open. She'd lost her way trying to find her locker after lunch and had only two minutes to get to her math class. The locker finally opened, and Lauren searched in it for the school map. She wasn't sure where her math classroom was.

A sea of unfamiliar faces moved past her, flowing quickly to fifth period before the bell rang—but no one stopped to ask Lauren if she needed help. Lauren leaned against her locker. Her last school had only twenty class-rooms situated in two hallways. She knew everyone there and considered most friends.

"If only I were back at Lincoln," she thought. "I'll never make friends here—I'll never even learn my way around school!"

YOUR TURN!

Starting at a new school is difficult for most students. Whether you graduate from elementary to middle school, move across the country, or move to a new school zone in your city, it means change. Preparing ahead can help. This chapter will help you do that.

GATHER INFORMATION

If you discover you are moving, find out all you can about your new location. You can find out most of what you need to know on the Web. Type in the city and state, and you'll find Web sites for the chamber of commerce or parks and recreation department. If you prefer, you can actually write a letter to the chamber of commerce for information.

Find the Web site for the school district. It will show you which school you will attend, what bus to ride, and where to meet it. It will give you the dress code, sports schedules, extra-curricular activity list, and maybe even the school lunch menu!

Here is a list of some things you might want to know about your new location:

- ★ **Is the area city or rural?**

- ★ **Is the city large or small?**

- ★ **How many schools are there?**

- ★ **What attractions are nearby?**

- ★ **What is the weather like year round?**

- ★ **How many malls are there?** Bowling alleys? Skating rinks?

- ★ **What sports are played in the city?**

Here is a list of some things you might want to know about your new school:

- ★ **What classes are offered?**

- ★ **How much choice do you have in selecting classes?**

- ★ **What clubs are offered?**

- ★ **What social activities do they have?**

- ★ **What committees can you serve on?**

- ★ **What sports do they offer?**

- ★ **Is there a school newspaper? Yearbook?**

- ★ **Are there musical or dramatic groups that perform?**

- ★ **Is there a dress code or uniforms?**

If you are entering middle school in the same school district where you attended elementary school, you may be given a tour of the middle school along with an information packet. If not, request both. Ask about orientation for incoming students.

FIND A CONTACT

If you're moving from elementary to middle school, you may have an older brother or sister who attends the middle school. If so, arrange to go to school with him or her the first day. If you don't have older brothers or sisters, search the neighborhood for someone who attends the school.

If you've moved to a new city, you may not have met anyone yet. Look around your church for students your age. Some of them may attend the same school you will. Call the school and ask if there are student volunteers to help new students find their way. Many schools have this kind of program or would be willing to pair you up with a partner for the first day.

VISIT THE SCHOOL

If possible, visit the school before your first day and request a tour. If you know what classes you will take, find out the room numbers. Jot down notes, and plan your route. Meet the teachers, if you can. Locate your locker and practice the combination. Be sure to locate the gym, band room, rest rooms, and cafeteria.

SEEK OUT A FRIEND

Find another new student or someone you recognize

from your neighborhood or church youth group. Look for someone who's eating alone in the cafeteria or sitting alone in the library. Approach the student. Take a risk. You may make a life-long friend!

First Day Tips

Have all your supplies.
If you don't have a supply list, take the things you know you'll need, such as paper, pens, pencils, calculator, highlighters, folders, and a ruler.

Be organized.
Have a planner, map, and schedule in hand.

Start well rested.
Sleep a full eight hours the night before.

Start with a good breakfast, even if your stomach feels jittery.

Be positive.
Don't complain, even if you miss everything about your old school.

Just Do It!

Are you facing a new school? Find out the answer to these questions:

How many students attend the school?

What are the school colors?

What is the team name?

What is the mascot?

Do they have a newspaper and yearbook?

Do they have band, orchestra, and choir?

Did they perform any plays or musicals last year?

What elective classes are offered?

What clubs do they have?

What sports do they offer?

Write down which of the classes, clubs, activities, and sports interest you. Consider trying something new.

1.

2.

3.

4.

5.

Arrange for a tour of the school. Find out the answers to these questions:

Where is your locker located?

What is the room number of your homeroom?

Where is the cafeteria?

Where is the gym?

Where is the library?

Where are the rest rooms?

List the room number of your classroom for each period if you know them.

First _____

Second _____

Third _____

Fourth _____

Fifth _____

Sixth _____

VERSES TO THINK ABOUT

It is the Lord who goes before you. He will be with you; He will not leave you or forsake you. Do not fear or be dismayed. **Deuteronomy 31:8**

_____

For He has said, "I will never leave you nor forsake you." **Hebrews 13:5b**

_____

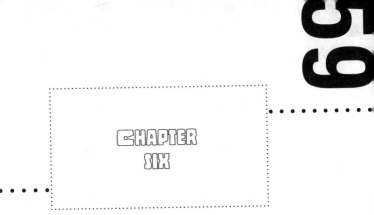

CHAPTER SIX

Here a Friend, There a Friend

Do you have one or more close friends? Do you meet people easily? Whether you've started at a new school or could just use another friend or two, this chapter will give you ideas for forming new friendships.

Samantha sat at the lunch table, her food tray untouched. She watched groups of students talking and laughing all around her. "I wish I was part of one of those groups," Samantha thought. "I wonder how it would feel not to eat lunch alone every day."

Samantha wasn't unfriendly, but she was shy. It was hard for her to approach new

people and make friends. She had lots of friends on the Internet, but few in real life and none at school.

Samantha stabbed her fork into her salad. She looked around, hoping to see someone else alone, but everyone was caught up in lively discussions. She wondered how she'd survive the school year without anyone to talk to.

YOUR TURN!

Making friends is easy for some students and harder for others. Which group do you fall into? Whether you make friends easily or are more like Samantha, this chapter has some tips for you.

HOW WELL DO YOU MAKE NEW FRIENDS?

Take the quiz below to find out how well you make new friends. Read each sentence and circle the answer that best describes you.

1. There's a new kid at school today. You see him sitting alone at lunch. You

    a. sit with your own group of friends.

    b. hope someone will sit with him, you wouldn't know what to say.

    c. sit with him.

    d. ask him to join your group.

2. During free time at the end of lunch, everyone goes outside to talk and hang out. You

> a. meet your group in your normal spot.
>
> b. read a book.
>
> c. find someone who's not in a group to talk with.
>
> d. look around for some others to join your fun.

3. Everyone in your homeroom is invited to a birthday at the skating rink this Saturday. You

> a. go together with your friends.
>
> b. skip it. You're not good with parties.
>
> c. go alone and hope you won't spend the whole afternoon skating by yourself.
>
> d. go and plan to meet up with others there.

4. A new player shows up for basketball practice. You:

> a. warm up with your friends same as always.
>
> b. continue warming up by yourself.
>
> c. invite the new player to join you warming up one-on-one.
>
> d. include the new player in your group.

5. You just walked into your school for the first time. You

> a. wait for a group.
>
> b. concentrate on finding your first class.
>
> c. look for a friendly face, smile, and say "hi."
>
> d. find some friendly looking students to join.

How did you do?

Mostly A's: You are comfortable with your best friend or group of friends. You're not looking for new friends at this time. Try to look outside your group. There may be another student in need of a friend or who would be a perfect friend for you. Be careful not to become part of a clique.

Mostly B's: You are often alone. Whether you're shy or just don't want to take a risk, you aren't going to make new friends unless you take the initiative and talk to others around you. You may be surprised.

Mostly C's: You may often be alone, but you are on the lookout for a new friend. You may need to step out of your comfort zone and make the first move. Smile and say "hi."

Mostly D's: You have your own group of friends but you are willing to welcome a new student to the group. You are confident in your friendship abilities and enjoy making new friends.

Not sure how to get started making new friends? Try some of these ideas.

KNOW WHAT YOU'RE LOOKING FOR

Friends have a big influence on you, so it's important to consider what kind you want. What are you looking for? What is most important—a sense of humor? Popularity? Strong values? Loyalty?

Make a list of your own beliefs, values, and interests. How will these affect your friendships? For instance, you may want a friend who goes to your church or one who shares your love of reading. Or maybe truthfulness and dependability are more important to you. Deciding what you want in a friendship ahead of time will help you know when you've found a good friend.

A real friend shares both good times and bad. Real friends care about and help each other. David and Jonathan are well-known Bible friends. "Jonathan became one in spirit with David, and he loved him as himself" (1 Samuel 18:1 NIV). True friends care about others as well as themselves. Don't settle for less!

GO WHERE THERE ARE OTHER MIDDLE SCHOOL STUDENTS

Sitting at home won't help you make friends. Be in contact with others your age—the kind you want to get to know. Here are some places where you might meet other middle school students:

★ **Youth group**

★ **City youth rallies**

★ **School Bible studies and clubs**

★ **Special-interest clubs**

★ **Sports teams or events**

★ **Newspaper or yearbook staff**

★ **Tutoring programs**

★ **Choir or pep band**

★ **Ministry programs**

★ **Volunteer organizations**

BE FRIENDLY TO EVERYONE

If you set your sights only on making friends with the in crowd, you may set yourself up for disappointment or find that you are tempted to compromise values and beliefs in order to fit in. Be friendly to everyone, and pray that God will bring the friend you need. It may be the quiet math whiz, the person who sits behind you in science, or someone you meet at the library. Be open to different personalities and individuals, but be true to your beliefs.

MAKE THE FIRST MOVE

Don't wait for others to find you. If you are in a big school, you may never be noticed! Say "hi" to those sitting near you in each of your classes. Find out people's names and use them. Ask about their other classes, church, or family. Try to find common interests. You will soon have an idea of which classmates would be interesting to know. Invite them over to do homework or study for a test together. Ask them to a youth group party or activity. Let them know you are interested in being their friend.

BE A GOOD LISTENER

Encourage others to talk about themselves. Really listen to them for clues to hobbies, interests, problems, and values. Listen to the meaning as well as the words. You may learn more by a tone of voice and body language than by what's actually said. Listen for the underlying emotions, fears, or joy.

Remember what is important to your new friend and ask more about it later. This will let the person know you were really listening.

BE DEPENDABLE

Do what you say you will, when you say you will. If you plan to meet at the mall at 7:00, be there at 7:00. People need friends they can count on. If you get into the habit of not showing up or not calling when you say you will, you'll soon have a reputation for being unreliable.

Your friends also need to be able to depend on you to stick with them in difficult times. No one needs a friend who can't be counted on.

BE COURTEOUS

No one wants to be with someone who is rude or ignores the basics of appropriate behavior. Your everyday manners say a lot about you. Interrupting, being loud, and dominating conversations turn people away quickly. Think of others, and let their interests and needs be as important as your own.

BE UPBEAT AND POSITIVE

It's hard not to be friends with someone who is genuine, warm, and enthusiastic. This isn't to say that you can't share the tough times with your friends, but few people want to hang out with someone who is constantly complaining or blue. Learn to be joyful inside, and it will show on the outside.

TAKE YOUR TIME

Don't try to rush friendships—they take time to develop. Trying to get too close too fast makes you appear pushy or clingy. Watch for clues as to how fast the other person wants the friendship to develop too.

ACCEPT REJECTION

Not everyone will like you. Don't let this hurt you or keep you from trying again. Popularity doesn't reflect on your self-worth. Some personalities just don't fit well together. Use times of rejection to evaluate your life and improve yourself if needed. Then go on and try again.

These steps can help you form new friendships this school year.

LOSING FRIENDS

Making friends is only half the battle. Keeping them requires effort on your part too. You can quickly lose friends with these friendship killers:

- ★ **Neglecting your friend when someone better comes along.**

- ★ **Borrowing clothes, homework, and social standing.**

- ★ **Being negative, whining, and complaining.**

- ★ **Dominating conversations with stories about yourself.**

- ★ **Being envious of your friends' money, talents or grades.**

- ★ **Gossiping about your friends.**

- ★ **Being critical of your friends' other friends.**

- ★ **Unloading your problems on your friends but being too busy to listen to their problems.**

★ Displaying jealousy when a friend spends time with other friends.

★ Trying to top everything your friends do.

Making friends is an important part of school. If you work on being a good friend and avoid the friendship killers, you can form lasting friendships during your school years.

Just Do It!

Do you want to make new friends? Ask God to help you be the friend you should and bring the right friends to you.

What beliefs, values, and interests do you want your friends to share? List them in order with the most important at the top.

1.

2.

3.

4.

5.

Conversation Starters

Don't know what to talk about? Here are some questions to get the conversation started.

Do you have any bothers or sisters?

How old are they?

Which one do you get along with best? fight with most?

What is your best subject?

Who is your favorite teacher?

What do you do after school?

Do you play any sports?

What's your favorite television show?

What kind of music do you listen to?

What church do you go to?

If you don't go to church, would you like to visit mine?

Where can you go to meet others who share your values and interests? List below.

1.

2.

3.

4.

5.

What strengths do you have to offer a friendship—loyalty, a listening ear, a sense of humor, etc.? List the traits you hope others will see in you.

1.

2.

3.

4.

5.

Look around you this week. Are there potential friends? Introduce yourself. Listen as they talk and take steps toward cultivating friendships.

VERSES TO THINK ABOUT

A friend loves at all times, and a brother is born for adversity. **Proverbs 17:17**

A man of many companions may come to ruin, but there is a friend who sticks closer than a brother. **Proverbs 18:24**

Living Your Faith at School

Whether you are in a public, private, charter, or Christian school, there are challenges. One of those is living out your faith consistently each day—and sharing it with others. This chapter will give you ideas for sharing your faith in the classroom.

Victor paused at the front steps of Washington Middle School. It was his first day as a student there and he wasn't sure what to expect. Would there be other Christians? Would he have a chance to share his faith—or courage to do so? Would the classroom discussions conflict with his beliefs?

Victor hoped that there would be some kind of Bible club or Christian athletes' club at the school, or that at least he would see someone from church. But he knew that didn't always make a difference; sometimes the kids from church were the worst of all.

"God, help me face whatever is ahead," Victor prayed silently. "Give me the courage to hold onto my faith and share it with others."

He pulled the door open and entered, feeling like Daniel on the way to the lions' den.

YOUR TURN!

Sharing your faith doesn't have to be scary; it can be a natural part of life. Whether you are outgoing or shy, part of a crowd or a loner, you can be a witness in the classroom.

WHAT'S YOUR STYLE?

Your personality, talents, and fear factor determine how you live out your faith at school. What's your style? Take this quiz to find out. Circle the answer that sounds most like you.

1. A friend said something that hurt your feelings. You

    a. talk about classes, the weekend, and everything else before bringing it up—if you do bring it up at all.

    b. confront the friend up front about what he did to hurt your feelings.

    c. let it go; you don't want to stir up trouble.

    d. plan precisely what to say before confronting the friend.

2. When attending a party, what are you most likely to do?

    a. Join in the fun.

    b. Take over and organize the fun.

    c. Hang loose and see what happens.

    d. Stay back and observe.

3. What are you doing for your science project?

    a. A group presentation

    b. A presentation by yourself

    c. Whatever your parents help you think up

    d. A detailed written report

4. You've been asked to help at Vacation Bible School. You volunteer to

    a. do a skit or lead singing.

    b. teach the lesson.

    c. sit with the children to keep them quiet.

    d. keep attendance records.

5. People would describe you as

    a. fun

    b. determined

    c. easy going

    d. prepared

How did you do?

Count up how many you have of each letter.

Mostly A's: You are friendly and outgoing. You like being with people and having fun. It's not hard for you to talk to people, so sharing your faith may be easy, especially if you can do it in an entertaining way such as through a skit or presentation. It's also easy for you to invite your friends to church. Just make sure you pick them up or meet them there. Not everyone is outgoing, and new places intimidate some people. You are like the Apostle Peter, who was brave when he remembered to trust in Jesus, not in his own power.

Mostly B's: You are direct and outspoken. It's easy for you to share your opinion. Be careful of people's feelings, though. You sometimes ignore other people's opinions while giving your own. Because of your tendency to be direct, it's not hard for you to share your faith. You could do so as part of a persuasive speech or other oral presentation. You are similar to the Apostle Paul, who boldly shared his faith.

Mostly C's: You are calm and easygoing. You are easy to get along with and are the peacemaker among your friends. You tend to be cautious and may not make decisions easily. You aren't as outgoing as some of the students around you, so you may share your faith in a more quiet or private way, such as talking to students one-on-one or counseling a friend with a problem. You may be like Abraham, who was known for his faith but had to be nudged by God to get started.

Mostly D's: You are a loyal friend, but you don't mind spending time alone. You think things through, and they need to make sense to you. Those around you may find you moody. You like your work to be precise and detailed. You aren't a natural leader, but are capable of it. You share your faith in an organized and logical way. You may be similar to Moses, who did not want a leadership position, but God chose him and used him anyway.

SHARING YOUR FAITH ONE-ON-ONE

You don't have to be a missionary or preacher to share your faith; you just need the desire. These suggestions will help you get started.

★ **Live a consistent Christian life.** Your friends watch your actions. Displaying a bad attitude, swearing, cheating, or goofing around in class will not point the way to God.

★ **Invite your friends to your church's youth activities.** Even if they won't attend church, they may attend a sports night or pizza party. Be specific in your invitation. Instead of asking, "Do you want to go to youth group with me sometime?" ask, "Would you like to come to our youth group game night Friday night? I'll pick you up at 7:00." People respond quicker to a specific invitation.

★ **Loan your favorite Christian fantasy or suspense novel to a classmate.**

★ **Offer encouragement to a discouraged friend and share a favorite Scripture.**

★ **Give greeting cards with a Christian message.**

LIVING YOUR FAITH IN THE CLASSROOM

Sometimes you'll have the chance to share your faith in the classroom. This doesn't mean standing on your chair and waving your Bible in the air, but planting the seeds of faith through well-thought-out statements. Here are some things to remember when that time comes.

★ **Avoid confrontations.** If a teacher makes a comment conflicting with your beliefs, think before replying. Would this be the best time to say something? If so, what is the best way to convey your message?

★ **Have a positive attitude.** Arguing, getting mad, condemning others, or having a bad attitude about schoolwork won't help you portray victorious Christian living. Be positive, mature, and in control.

★ **Don't refuse to answer questions or do homework.** If a test question conflicts with your beliefs, don't refuse to answer it. You might say, "The textbook states that . . ." If you receive a homework assignment that involves reading or watching something inappropriate, talk to the teacher about an alternative assignment. If you get no results, talk to your parents about the situation.

★ **Include Christianity in your schoolwork whenever possible.** Here are some ideas:

Write a history report on the Reformation, the persecution of the Early Church, or another event from Church history. Or focus on the part Christianity played in the life of a person, such as Martin Luther King Jr., Christopher Columbus, or Joan of Arc.

Write a book report for English on the biography of a great man or woman of faith, such as Amy Carmichael, James Hudson Taylor, C.S. Lewis, or John Bunyan. Or choose a novel by a Christian author and encourage others to read it.

Choose a science project that points to God's hand in nature or the laws of science. Make the presentation outstanding!

These ideas will make sharing your faith with friends and in your classroom a natural way of life for you.

Just Do It!

Are you ready to share your faith? Let's get started!

What is your style according to the quiz? Does it fit you? How are you like the Bible character mentioned?

List friends that you could share your faith with. What would be the best way to do it?

Friend   **Idea**

Look for ways to share your faith in the classroom and your schoolwork. What current assignments could allow you to share your faith?

Before I formed you in the womb I knew you, before you were born I set you apart; I appointed you as a prophet to the nations. **Jeremiah 1:5 (NIV)**

And I am sure of this, that He who began a good work in you will bring it to completion at the day of Jesus Christ. **Philippians 1:6**

But in your hearts honor Christ the Lord as holy, always being prepared to make a defense to anyone who asks you for a reason for the hope that is in you; yet do it with gentleness and respect. **1 Peter 3:15**

CHAPTER
EIGHT

On the Mend

Have you drifted away from elementary school friends? Do you face more complex problems in your middle school friendships? Both of these things are common. This chapter looks at some friendship problems and how to fix them.

Matthew and Christopher were friends throughout elementary school. Both were considered class clowns, although they made satisfactory grades. Both enjoyed sports. They'd shoot baskets for hours in the evening and played on a church basketball team together. On Sunday afternoons, they would watch football on television.

Once Matthew and Christopher started seventh grade, things begin to change. Matthew got serious about his schoolwork,

but Christopher continued his role as class clown. Matthew tried out for the school basketball team and made it, but Christopher didn't want to commit to that many hours of practice after school. He started going to another friend's house after school to play electronic games instead.

Suddenly Matthew and Christopher weren't best friends any more. They were hardly friends at all. Both had changed and, as a result, they drifted apart.

YOUR TURN!

All friendships have rough times. Sometimes these can end a friendship. Other times friends just drift apart like Matthew and Christopher. Do you have a friendship that's suffering? Are you willing to work at repairing it? Good friendships are worth it!

THINK ABOUT YOUR FRIENDSHIP

Consider the reasons your friendship first formed. Were you on a sports team together or assigned to the same group for a project? Are you neighbors or in the same youth group? Do you share common interests?

How do you feel now? Do you enjoy spending time together? Are your interests similar? Considering these things will help you decide if a friendship is worth saving.

WHEN FRIENDS GROW APART

Friends may drift apart over time. An elementary school

friendship dwindles in middle school. Your closest buddy now seems distant. There are many reasons for this:

- ★ **You develop different interests.**

- ★ **You make new friends.**

- ★ **You are in conflict over values.**

- ★ **You mature at different rates.**

- ★ **You have separate schedules or schools.**

It is natural to form new friendships over time. This differs from friendships that end abruptly due to a fight or misunderstanding.

FRACTURED FRIENDSHIPS

Misunderstandings, betrayal of trust, and disagreements can end friendships. A friend might tell a secret you trusted her with or you might find yourselves disagreeing on what to do each weekend. When a problem threatens a relationship, determine to work at resolving it and restoring the friendship. Ask yourself, "Is the problem solvable and the relationship worth saving?" If so, it can be mended.

MENDING FRACTURED FRIENDSHIPS

Determine to take steps toward fixing the friendship, whether or not the conflict was your fault.

> ★ **Think about the problem.** What went wrong? What feelings, motives, or disagreements played a part? Could it have been handled another way with different results?

★ **Talk it out.** Arrange a time for the two of you talk alone. State your feelings in a positive way. Avoid criticism or cutdowns. Ask God for wisdom in choosing your words.

★ **Listen with an open mind.** Hear your friend out. You may be viewing the situation with two different perspectives. When you thought your friend was ignoring you at the party, he was only trying to reach out to a new peer. Or when you felt your friend was being clingy, she was displaying insecurity. Listen to your friend's words and the feeling behind them. Ask questions to clarify the situation. Let God guide you as you listen and talk.

★ **Accept blame.** Swallow your pride and admit any wrongdoing. Be honest about your feelings, conduct, and motives. Forgive your friend whether or not the friend accepts blame or apologizes. Holding a grudge wears you down.

★ **Leave it behind.** If you are able to restore the friendship, leave the hurts behind. Don't bring them up later.

★ **Let go.** In spite of all you do, your friendship may end. If differences are too great to reconcile or values too different, let go gracefully. You still have memories of shared times. Treasure these and pray for your friend. Use what you've learned from this friendship to build a new, stronger friendship with someone else. What you've learned through difficulties may make you a better friend later.

Most friendships have a few bumps and bruises along the way. Usually they are overcome and the friendship strengthened. Work on patching up the friendships in your life.

CAN THE FRIENDSHIP BE SAVED?

Check yes or no for each question below.

1. My friend and I share the same values.

____ Yes ____ No

2. We have more in common than different.

____ Yes ____ No

3. We can usually talk out our problems.

____ Yes ____ No

4. I am willing to accept the blame for my part of the problem.

____ Yes ____ No

5. My friend and I bring out the best in each other.

____ Yes ____ No

6. I feel the friendship is worth fixing.

____ Yes ____ No

If you marked mostly *yes*, then the friendship can be saved.

★ **Be willing to talk and listen.**

★ **Be honest about your feelings.**

★ **Determine what went wrong and work through it.**

If you marked mostly *no*, the friendship is in danger. Are you sure you want to save it?

★ **Do you have enough in common to maintain a friendship?**

★ **Will conflicts over values or faith put a strain on the relationship?**

★ **Does this friend build you up and enrich your life?**

If not, there may be a better friend for you. Be friendly, and ask God to bring the right friends to you.

Just Do It!

Evaluate your friendships. Have they suffered from misunderstandings, hurt, feelings of betrayal, or even unkind words?

★ **Set a time to talk.** Stop and call your friend now.

★ **Evaluate the problem.** When did the problem start? What caused it? How can you best share your feelings with your friend?

★ **How could the situation have been handled differently?** What could you have done?

List ways to keep the problem from reoccurring and ways to strengthen your relationship:

★ **Evaluate the friendship.** What strengths do each of you bring to the friendship?

Friend: **Idea:**

In what ways do you strengthen and enrich each other?

If you can't think of any ways in which your friend adds to your life, challenges you to be stronger in your faith and do your best, then it might be time to look elsewhere for friendship.

VERSES TO THINK ABOUT

Do nothing from rivalry or conceit, but in humility count others more significant than yourselves. Let each of you look not only to his own interests, but also to the interests of others. Have this mind among yourselves, which is yours in Christ Jesus.
Philippians 2:3–5

Be kind to one another, tenderhearted, forgiving one another, as God in Christ forgave you.
Ephesians 4:32

Choose the Best

Do you wonder what activities you should be involved in? Is it hard to figure out what a Christian should and should not do? This chapter presents principles to guide you in making the best choices.

> Jeremy studied the poster on the school bulletin board. Everyone was talking about the big concert Friday night. His friend Kyle walked up and read the poster. "Wow, a free concert at the civic center? I'm not going to miss this! You're going, aren't you?"
>
> "I don't know. Some of their music is okay, but some of it talks about things I don't agree with," Jeremy said.

Jeremy sat thinking on his bed that night. "I really don't think I should go—but everyone else is going. Even the Christian teens are excited about it. I don't want to be left out or have people think I'm 'different.' Why are these decisions always so hard?"

YOUR TURN!

Are you facing some tough decisions? As a middle schooler, you make choices every day. You decide what to wear to school, what to eat for breakfast, what classes to take at school, what clubs to join, what sports to play, where to volunteer, and more. While the Bible doesn't give us a specific list of right and wrong activities for today's middle school student, it does give us principles to help us make the best choices. Four principles are found in 1 Corinthians.

CHOOSE ACTIVITIES THAT ARE HELPFUL

"'All things are lawful for me,' but not all things are help-ful" (1 Corinthians 6:12a). Sometimes an activity, although not bad in itself, serves no real purpose. Watching television, texting friends, and playing on a game system aren't bad in themselves, but why not choose activities that challenge you or build you up mentally, physically, or spiritually?

Try one of these:

★ Learn a new sport, such as handball or tennis.

★ Take up an aerobic exercise, such as biking or rollerblading.

★ Learn to cook Chinese or Creole food.

★ Play a game, such as chess or Stratego, to challenge your mind.

★ Try a game, such as Outburst or Apples to Apples, for family fun.

★ Learn a new hobby, such as photography or flower arranging, that could lead to a future job.

★ Take a water safety class.

★ Join the math or Spanish club.

★ Write or take pictures for your school paper or yearbook.

★ Take part in a church ministry.

★ Start a new Bible study.

CHOOSE ACTIVITIES THAT WON'T CONTROL YOU

"'All things are lawful for me,' but I will not be enslaved by anything" (1 Corinthians 6:12b). Some activities start out as harmless recreation but end up as addictions. Sports is one example. You might become involved in a sport for fun and recreation, but it soon dominates your thoughts. Nothing matters more than succeeding in or watching that sport. It is constantly on your mind and begins ruling your life. The same thing can happen in other areas, such as these:

★ **Watching television**

★ **Listening to music**

★ **Playing arcade games**

* **Playing game systems**

* **Participation in a club or hobby**

* **Studying**

While the activity in itself isn't bad, if it controls your time, money, or thoughts, it's time to look for something new.

CHOOSE ACTIVITIES
THAT STRENGTHEN YOU PHYSICALLY

"Or do you not know that your body is a temple of the Holy Spirit within you, whom you have from God? You are not your own, for you were bought with a price. So glorify God in your body" (1 Corinthians 6:19–20). Some things are obviously harmful to your body, such as smoking, drinking, and taking drugs. But most of us are guilty of staying up too late, eating too much, or neglecting to exercise. Too much exercise can also have a negative effect on your body. Follow these guidelines to keep your body in maximum physical shape:

* **Get at least eight hours of sleep a night—nine is better.**

* **Eat three well-balanced meals each day.**

* **Choose healthy snacks, such as fruit or low-fat yogurt.**

* **Drink lots of water, especially in hot weather or when exercising.**

* **Participate in an aerobic sport, such as biking, running, or skateboarding, for at least a half hour three times a week.**

CHOOSE ACTIVITIES THAT GLORIFY GOD

"So, whether you eat or drink, or whatever you do, do all to the glory of God" (1 Corinthians 10:31). Do others know you are a Christian by your actions? Christians are responsible for bringing honor to God's name. If you are participating in activities that weaken your faith walk or Christian witness, it's time for a change. Choose activities that point others to Christ or show them a more abundant lifestyle. Not all of your activities need to be spiritual in nature, but they should be above reproach. How would you feel if God walked into your room while you and your best friends were participating in your favorite activities? Would your activities get His stamp of approval?

Use these four principles to help you choose the best activities—ones that are beneficial and not addictive, activities that build you up physically and are pleasing to God.

Just Do It!

List your favorite activities below. Include sports, hobbies, clubs, church activities, and social times.

1.

2.

3.

4.

5.

6.

7.

8.

9.

10.

Reread each item you listed. Decide if it is physically, mentally, emotionally, or spiritually beneficial. Put a *P*, *M*, *E*, or *S* after each one to indicate in what area it benefits you. Some items may be beneficial in more than one area, and some in no area. Reconsider the latter. Are there other activities you could replace them with?

Of the items you listed, do any of them control you? Do they control your time, thoughts, or money? Put a *T* after any activity that dominates your time, *TH* for thoughts, and $ for money. Rethink these activities. How can you change their hold on your life? Is it time to replace them with new activities?

Do the activities build you up physically? Do any of them harm your body? Circle any that have a negative effect on you physically. Decide how to change or replace those activities.

Of the activities listed, would any of them bring you shame if God walked in and saw you participating in them? Do the activities portray victorious living in Christ?

You have many activities to choose from. Consider the principles given and choose only the best activities.

VERSES TO THINK ABOUT

I came that they may have life and have it abundantly. **John 10:10b**

"All things are lawful for me," but not all things are helpful. "All things are lawful for me," but I will not be enslaved by anything. **1 Corinthians 6:12**

So, whether you eat or drink, or whatever you do, do all to the glory of God. **1 Corinthians 10:31**

Do you not know that your body is a temple of the Holy Spirit within you, whom you have from God? You are not your own, for you were bought with a price. So glorify God in your body. **1 Corinthians 6:19–20**

CHAPTER
TEN

Stand Up!

Are you faced with negative peer pressure? Do you wish it was easier to do what is right? This chapter will show you how to exert peer pressure of your own.

> *Emily watched as Sarah and Taylor logged in to the chat room. She didn't really like to spend that much time online, but she knew most other middle school students did. Sarah and Taylor were constantly talking about how cool it was.*
>
> *"What do you think?" Sarah asked Emily. "Do you want to create a user name and join in?"*
>
> *"I don't know. Maybe next time," Emily said.*
>
> *"Oh, come on. You're the only who doesn't*

like to do social networking," Taylor said. "We'll help you get started."

"Okay," Emily agreed. She didn't want to be in a chat room. She would rather be doing something else like listening to music or shooting baskets. Emily wondered why she always did what Sarah and Taylor wanted to do, not what she liked.

YOUR TURN!

Do you find yourself giving in to what your friends want you to do? Maybe they talk you into an activity that you don't really like. Or maybe they get you to do things you know are wrong. This chapter will help you identify the peer pressure in your life and stand against it.

REALIZE THE POWER OF PEER INFLUENCE

Everyone is influenced by friends. It's not wrong to wear popular clothing or shoes as long as they don't send a message contrary to Christian teachings or distract others from their Christian faith. . It's natural to want to fit in with the group, and that's fine as long as they share your values and beliefs.

But how often are you doing things your friends want you to do rather than the things you want to do? Do you give in to things you feel are wrong rather than stand up for what is right? Take the quiz below to find out how well you handle peer pressure. Circle the answer that sounds most like you.

1. Your friends are all going to join the tutoring program. Tutoring others is a great thing to do, but it's not something you're dying to do. What will you do?

  a. Go along so you won't look bad for not helping out.

  b. Decide to do it because you don't have anything better to do.

  c. Join another worthwhile group that more fits your talents.

2. You wear a new jacket to school. You like it, but a couple of the cool kids pretend to gag and point at it as you walk by. What will you do?

  a. Stick it in the back of your closet and never wear it again.

  b. Give it to your little sister—she likes it better than you do anyway.

  c. Wear it again because you like it.

3. A classmate finds an answer key for tomorrow's math test on the floor under the teacher's desk. He quickly writes down the answers and passes the paper to another friend. It's coming to you next. What will you do?

  a. Write down the answers. Why should you have to study more than the others?

  b. Just take a quick peek as you pass it on.

  c. Give it back to the first person and encourage him to return it.

4. A new girl comes to class. Her clothes and hair are outdated. She seems lost and out of place. The others snicker and roll their eyes. What will you do?

a. Laugh along with them. After all, she has to know she's wearing out-of-date styles.

b. Ignore the situation.

c. Offer to show her around the school.

5. A friend tells you he's found a pack of cigarettes and plans to smoke one later. He asks a bunch of guys, including you, if they want to try one too. What will you do?

a. Agree. You've always wondered what smoking would be like and this one puff won't hurt.

b. Go with them but don't smoke. You just don't want to be left out.

c. Tell them "no thanks." A smoking habit starts with a single cigarette.

How did you do?

Mostly A's: You follow the crowd, even if it sometimes means going against your own desires or what's right. Wanting to be like others is okay—as long as they make good choices.

Mostly B's: You don't always go along with the crowd, but you don't stand up for yourself either. Sometimes doing nothing makes people assume you agree with what they are doing. Speak up for yourself.

Mostly C's: You do what's right, and you don't give up what you want just to fit in. You don't mind following the crowd if they are doing the right thing, but you aren't afraid to say "no."

TAKE YOUR STAND

Here are some ideas:

★ **Seek friends who are a positive influence.**
Friends play an important role in our lives. They influence how we act, talk, and dress; what activities we participate in; and even what television shows we watch. Choose friends who will build you up, encourage you to make good choices, and stand with you when the going is tough. Look for others who are involved in wholesome activities and will support you in doing the same.

★ **Stand up for right.** There are many students who want to do the right thing but are too timid to speak out. Be the first to stand up and say no to wrong. You don't have to campaign in the school hallways, just look for opportunities to put in a positive word. When a conversation turns to wrong things, speak out for your beliefs.

★ **Seek out positive groups and clubs.** Look for organizations such as student groups against alcohol, drugs, or abortion, or for Christian organizations and clubs. Investigate programs such as peer tutoring or mentoring. Be a part of organizations where you can make a difference and can have a positive influence in the life of a fellow student, your school, and your community.

★ **Find alternatives.** Sometimes it can be hard to stand up against negative peer pressure. If you feel that you can't do it alone, talk to a parent or pastor. And don't forget to talk to God about it.

Don't settle for just avoiding the negative; look for positive alternatives. There are a lot of fun and exciting activities to participate in. Chapter 11 will talk about creating activities for yourself and others.

Just Do It!

Consider your clothing, television viewing, leisure reading, activities, and even the way you talk. In what areas do others most influence you?

Is the influence a positive or negative force in your life?

Do you have friends who will support you in making a positive difference in your school? Are there other students who share your ideals? List ones you think would help exert positive peer pressure.

Talk to these students and share some of your ideas and goals. If they are interested, arrange to meet together to plan and pray.

Check the community page of your local paper or ask at your school office about organizations that are making a difference. Find out as much as you can about each. Choose ones that allow you to make a positive impact. List your ideas below.

VERSES TO THINK ABOUT

So, whether you eat or drink, or whatever you do, do all to the glory of God. **1 Corinthians 10:31**

Let no one despise you for your youth, but set the believers an example in speech, in conduct, in love, in faith, in purity. **1 Timothy 4:12**

Plan Your Own Activities

Are you tired of missing out on things because they aren't appropriate for Christians? Do you wish you had other activities to choose from? This chapter will help you create activities for yourself and your friends

> "Hey, Grady, did you hear about the big party Daniel's having next Friday?" Miguel asked.
>
> Grady turned to face him. "Who hasn't heard about it?"
>
> "Guess it's going to be the party of the year," Miguel said.

"Yeah, questionable activities and R-rated movies. Sorry; I'm not interested."

"I'm not really, either, but I get tired of missing out on everything," Miguel said.

"That's one party I'm not sorry to miss. He's going to be in trouble if his parents come home early. But I know what you mean about missing out. It's hard to find things to do that are both fun and acceptable. I wish we had more teens at church so we could do things together as a youth group," Grady said.

"So what are we going to do Friday night while everyone else is at Daniel's party?" Miguel asked.

Grady shrugged. "Probably stay home as usual. Maybe I'll start my science project."

YOUR TURN!

Do you find it hard to find fun activities that you are allowed to do? You don't have to sit at home. Create your own activities!

ENLIST THE HELP OF FRIENDS

Talk to friends and students in your classes. Check out their feelings about social activities. Are some of them having trouble finding appropriate activities? Would they help you plan fun things to do? Look for teens at church that might also be interested. Then hold a planning meeting to create fun and appropriate things to do. Invite everyone over for pizza.

Have pen and paper ready to make some plans.

LIST ALTERNATIVES

What social activities have taken place recently that you've had to miss because they weren't right for you? Are there activities coming up that you know you won't be going to? Think about activities to replace those. For instance, suppose your school is planning a Halloween party that centers around the occult, fortune-telling, and so on. Plan your own activity. Have an all-night video marathon, with everyone bringing favorite movies and snacks to share. Or, if your school is planning a big dance featuring one of the worst rock bands you've heard, plan a night out with your friends. Dress up and use the money you would have spent on the dance to go to a nice restaurant as a group.

Invite others to join you. Let them know you aren't trying to compete with the other event, just offering an alternative. You may form new friendships that will last beyond your school years.

TALK TO YOUR SCHOOL OFFICIALS

If school activities are repetitious, maybe it's time for a change. Suggest new activities for your school. For instance, offer to help plan a harvest festival instead of a Halloween party or a banquet instead of the usual dance. Be creative and invite others to help. You may be surprised at how many students are ready for a change.

PLAN CHURCH-RELATED ACTIVITIES

Talk with your youth leader about inappropriate school events. He may not realize the problem. Discuss the possibility of a monthly social event at church. Try something new each time. Have a pizza party and movie one month, go bowling or skating the next, and have a board-game marathon the next.

Plan creative activities too. Here are some ideas:

★ **Stuff night.** Divide into teams. See which team can stuff the most people into a phone booth, compact car, bathtub, and so on. Or, stuff things. For instance, see which team can stuff the most balloons in a bag without breaking any.

★ **Progressive dinner.** Meets at one person's house for appetizers. Then travel to another's house for salad and on to another for the main meal. Stop at the last house for dessert. Or you could do a fast-food progressive dinner. Go to Wendy's for salad, McDonald's for fries, Burger King for a burger, Sonic for a beverage, and Dairy Queen for ice cream.

★ **Game-Show Night.** Divide into teams for Family Feud, test your knowledge with Jeopardy, or play Deal or No Deal. Ask your grandparents about the show Let's Make a Deal and recreate that at your next get together.

★ **Theme Night.** Plan costumes, games, and food around a theme, such as Hawaiian, Olympics or sports teams.

Don't feel left out this year; plan creative, fun activities for you and your friends.

Just Do It!

List social activities that you've had to miss because they weren't appropriate for Christian students:

List possible alternatives:

List friends who would help you plan alternatives:

List ideas to present to your school officials or youth leader. Consider ideas for Halloween, Christmas, banquets, sports events, graduation trips and parties, and so on:

Smart Stuff

Do you struggle with math or language? Do you find that you do better at some subjects than others? You may not be a math genius or the top language student, but you are smart in one or more areas. This chapter will help you figure out what kind of smart you are.

> *Jacob looked at the math test in his hand. Another F! Why did school have to be so hard? It's not that he wasn't smart. He was smart about a lot of things. He could identify birds just by their call. He knew all the kinds of trees that grew in the woods behind his house. He could tell what animal had been there by looking at tracks. He just wasn't smart about stuff like reading and math.*

Jacob shoved the math paper to the bottom of his backpack. Maybe he could bring the grade up before report cards—but he doubted it. He'd probably be spending weekends with a math tutor again this year. He couldn't wait until he graduated, but that was still seven years away. He planned to be a forest ranger, and he hoped he wouldn't need math for that job.

YOUR TURN!

If you've ever felt like Jacob, this chapter is for you! You are smart stuff. If you feel like you have no talents or abilities and that you can't do anything right, don't worry. This chapter will help you discover your strong areas and how to make the most of them.

WHAT KIND OF SMART ARE YOU?

In the 1980s, a man named Howard Gardner wrote a famous book that said there are eight kinds of smart. He had the right idea. Not everyone excels in the same area. Take the quiz below to see what kind of smart you are. Circle the answers that describe you best. You can circle more than one answer for each question, but try not to circle too many or you won't be able to tell which are your best areas.

1. You have a mall gift certificate. What do you buy?

> A. Crossword puzzle book, Scrabble, and a new journal

B. Pocket planner, Stratego, and a new calculator

C. Complex book of mazes, art tablet and drawing pencils

D. New dance moves game, wood-burning set, and a soccer ball

E. CD by your favorite group, new music technique book, and sheet music for solo and ensemble competition

F. Scattergories, phone card, project to do with friends

G. Book of personality quizzes, journal, self-help book

H. Bird-watching book, binoculars, crystal-growing kit

2. What elective do you sign up for at school?

A. Journalism

B. Advanced math

C. Art

D. Personal fitness

E. Band or choir

F. Peer tutoring

G. Study hall

H. Astronomy

3. Your family is going on a trip. What would you do to help?

A. Keep a journal of your trip to send with the annual Christmas letter

B. Plan the best route

C. Take photographs

D. Plan activities for the rest stops

E. Pick the CDs to listen to

F. Be the peacekeeper (break up fights between siblings)

G. Daydream or start a private journal

H. Point out flowers, trees and animals along the way

4. What's your ideal field trip?

A. Newspaper office or television station

B. Science and technology museum

C. Art museum

D. Dance studio or baseball game

E. Concert or play performance

F. Pregnancy center or local Habitat for Humanity project

G. Library, individual project, scenic park

H. Wildlife sanctuary, planetarium, aquarium

5. Which of these jobs could you see yourself doing in the future?

A. Author, speaker, lawyer

B. Engineer, accountant, detective

C. Architect, graphics designer, photographer

D. Athlete, carpenter, actor

E. Singer, composer, instrumentalist

F. Teacher, counselor, youth pastor

G. Counselor, philosopher, performer

H. Botanist, biologist, environmentalist

Count how many A's you circled, how many B's and so on. Most people have a little ability in all of the areas. Many have two or three strong areas. You might find this true for you.

A's _____   D's _____   G's _____

B's _____   E's _____   H's _____

C's _____   F's _____

Mostly A's: You're word smart (Linguistic Intelligence). You like to read, write, and communicate by writing or speaking. You excel at word games and can master a foreign language.

Mostly B's: You're logic smart (Logical-Mathematical Intelligence). You find calculating numbers easy. Logic problems and reasoning come easily also. Patterns, sequences, and order make sense to you.

Mostly C's: You're picture smart (Visual-Spatial Intelligence). You can think in pictures and visualize things in your mind. You are quick to solve mazes because you see things in relationship to where they are to other objects. This makes you a good artist.

Mostly D's: You're body smart (Bodily-Kinesthetic Intelligence). You have excellent coordination and good fine- and large-motor skills. You quickly master new sports, and you enjoy dancing, acting, and making things with your hands.

Mostly E's: You're music smart (Musical Intelligence). You can compose music, play an instrument, sing, feel rhythm, and keep a beat. You can express yourself through rhythmic movement, composing, or performing music.

Mostly F's: You're people smart (Interpersonal Intelligence). You like to be with other people. You understand what makes your friends act the way they do. You empathize with others. You work well in groups and in role-playing.

Mostly G's: You're self-smart (Intrapersonal Intelligence). You understand your own feelings. You spend time alone thinking or journaling. You understand and learn from your accomplishments and failures.

Mostly H's: You're nature smart (Naturalist Intelligence). You quickly learn the names of things in nature. Everywhere you look, you see patterns in nature. You know how to use the earth and its resources productively.

USING YOUR STRONG AREAS

Did you find that you had one or more strong areas? The problem is that sometimes these don't reflect on your report card. But they are just as important as good grades for succeeding in life.

Do your best in all your classes, and when you get to choose electives, look for ones that match your abilities and interests.

Whenever you are assigned a project, put your smarts to work. Are you art smart? Ask if you can do your book report in pictures or comic strips. Are you body smart? Ask to act out your book report. Sometimes things have to be done in a certain way, but other times there might be room for creativity.

You can find other ways to put your talents to work. If you

are nature smart, you might create a terrarium for the science classroom. If you are art smart, offer to create graphics for the yearbook. If you are word smart, write for the school paper or write captions for the yearbook. If you are people smart, offer to mentor younger students.

If you struggle with knowing your strong areas or with how to put them to good use, talk to your school counselor, parent, or youth pastor. They can point you in the right direction.

Just Do It!

According to the quiz, what kind of smart are you? List the top two areas.

Do you agree?

What activities and interests do you already take part in that help you develop skills in that area?

How can you use those talents to help others?

How can you use them to serve God now and in the future?

VERSES TO THINK ABOUT

Before I formed you in the womb I knew you, before you were born I set you apart. **Jeremiah 1:5a (NIV)**

For I know the plans I have for you, declares the LORD, plans for welfare and not for evil, to give you a future and a hope. **Jeremiah 29:11**

Whatever you do, work heartily, as for the Lord and not for men. **Colossians 3:23**

Discussion Questions

CHAPTER ONE

1. Why is setting goals important?

2. How do you know God cares about your goals?

4. What is the importance of having a plan to achieve your goals?

5. How does checking your progress on your goals keep you on track?

CHAPTER TWO

1. What does it mean to be prepared for class?

2. In what way is listening more than just hearing words?

3. Do you use a school planner? How does it help you organize?

4. What can you do if you are having problems with a certain class?

CHAPTER THREE

1. Do you think you are a visual, auditory, or kinesthetic learner?

2. How can knowing this help you study?

3. Do you already use some of the ideas from this chapter when you study?

4. Explain your test-taking strategies.

5. Do you think that tests show what you truly know? Why or why not?

CHAPTER FOUR

1. Besides school and sleep, what takes up most of your time?

2. What method of planning your time (paper, calendar, electronic planner) works best for you?

3. Do you procrastinate a little, a lot, or not at all?

4. What is your biggest time waster? What can you do about it?

CHAPTER FIVE

1. Have you ever faced a new school?

2. How did you feel the first day?

3. What ways can you prepare for a new school?

4. What things do you most want to know about your new school?

5. How can you get that information?

CHAPTER SIX

1. Do you make new friends easily?

2. What characteristics are most important in a friend?

3. What do you have to offer in a friendship?

4. What advice do you have for someone who finds it difficult to make new friends?

CHAPTER SEVEN

1. According to the quiz, what's your style?

2. What ways do you share your faith at school?

3. Do you find it easy or difficult to live out your faith in the classroom? Why?

4. What assignments are coming up that you could use to share your faith?

CHAPTER EIGHT

1. What are some reasons that friends grow apart?

2. What would you do if you felt distant from a friend?

3. What things can end a friendship?

4. How can you tell when a friendship is worth saving?

CHAPTER NINE

1. What four things should you ask yourself about your activities?

2. Are there some activities that you should give up? Why?

3. Can you think of some activities that would benefit you spiritually? emotionally (socially)? intellectually? physically?

4. Can good activities ever become wrong?

CHAPTER TEN

1. In what areas are you most influenced by friends?

2. Is peer pressure good or bad? Why?

3. In what ways can you use positive peer pressure to change things at school?

4. What groups are you involved in that are making a difference?

CHAPTER ELEVEN

1. Do you have trouble finding appropriate activities, or does your church or school have activities available?

2. What activities do you feel uncomfortable taking part in?

3. What could you do instead?

CHAPTER TWELVE

1. What kind of smart are you?

2. Do you see this in your life?

3. What ways can you use it at school?

4. How can you build up that area of your life?